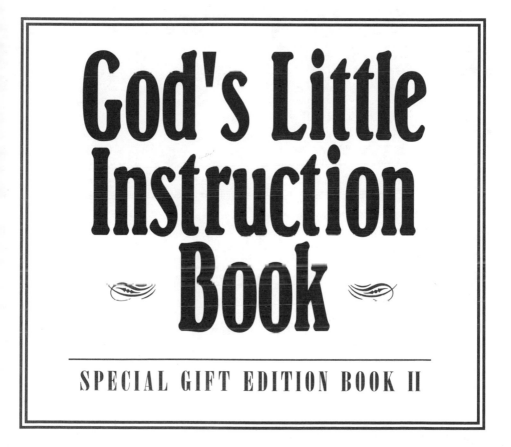

God's Little Instruction Book

SPECIAL GIFT EDITION BOOK II

2nd Printing
Over 151,000 in Print

God's Little Instruction Book II, Special Gift Edition
ISBN 1-56292-347-1
Copyright © 1994 by Honor Books, Inc.
P.O. Box 55388
Tulsa, Oklahoma 74155

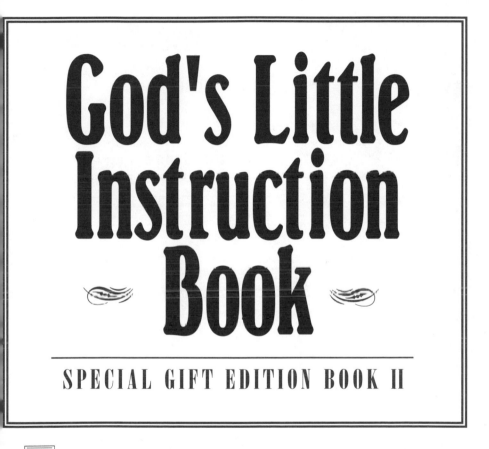

God's Little Instruction Book

SPECIAL GIFT EDITION BOOK II

Honor Books, Inc. • P.O. Box 55388 • Tulsa, OK 74155

Introduction

A number one bestseller deserves a sequel! We at Honor Books are proud to present *God's Little Instruction Book II, Special Gift Edition*. In the same fashion as the number one bestselling original, *God's Little Instruction Book II, Special Gift Edition* is an inspirational collection of quotes and Scriptures that will motivate you to live a meaningful, productive and happy life. This powerful little book combines both Scripture and quotes to provide not just man's insight, but also include the wisdom of the ages – God's Word.

Basic, practical and filled with the timeless wisdom of the Bible, this delightful book offers a road map to succeed in the daily journey of life. We here at Honor Books hope that you will learn to treasure *God's Little Instruction Book II, Special Gift Edition* as much as you have the original *God's Little Instruction Book*.

Acknowledgments

Oliver Wendell Holmes (8,137), Booker T. Washington (9), Ken S. Keyes, Jr. (10), Arnold H. Glasow (11,67,150), Mort Walker (12), Freeman (14), Ralph Waldo Emerson (16,65), Doug Larson (17,148), Peter Drucker (18), Richard Exley (19), J. Hudson Taylor (20), Morris Bender (22), Bernard Baruch (23), Norman Vincent Peale (24), Alistair Cooke (26), Larry Eisenberg (27), O. A. Battista (28), Charles Dickens (29), Charles Farr (32), Mark Twain (34,55,100), Elmer G. Letterman (36), C. Everett Koop (37), James Russell Lowell (38), Will Rogers (39), Robert Orben (41,63), John Buchan, Lord Tweedsmuir (43), Bern Williams (44), John Newton (45), Mark Steele (46), Hannah Moore (47), Winston Churchill (48), Michael LeBoeuf (49,54), John Locke (52), Boris Yeltsin (53), Waterloo (58), Alphonse Karr (62), Amos J. Farver (66), Olin Miller (70), Joseph P. Dooley (73), Andrew Carnegie (74), Dwight D. Eisenhower (76), Henry Ford (78), Thomas Chandler Haliburton (81), Leo Buscaglia (82), Margaret Thatcher (83), June Henderson (85), Dr. Jon Olson (86), Albert J. Nimeth (88), Jeremy Taylor (89), Josh Billings (90), Publilius Syrus (91), Grace Williams (92),

Cardinal Francis J. Spellman (94), P. T. Barnum (96), Mother Teresa (97), Rev. Larry Lorenzoni (99), Winston Churchill (103), Thomas Paine (104), James Howell (105), R.W. Emerson (106), Henry Ward Beecher (109), Charles Spurgeon (110,115,133), E.C. McKenzie (111), Anne Bradstreet (113), Dante Gabriel Rossetti (116), Thomas Jefferson (119), George W. Ford (121), Molly Ivins (122), Motley (123), Jim Elliot (124), Jim Patrick (125), Doug Larson (126), Elton Trueblood (127), Lawrence J. Peter (128), Mary Kay Ash (130), Tillotson (132), Billy Graham (134), James S. Sinclair (136), Ivern Ball (141), Parkes Robinson (142), C. L. Wheeler (144), Zig Ziglar (145), Lorene Workman (149), Mercelene Cox (150), John Mason (151), Fanuel Tjingaete (152), Dwight L. Moody (153), Malcolm Smith (154), Ernest Hemingway (158)

Choice, not chance, determines human destiny.

...I have set before you life and death, blessing and cursing: therefore choose life, that both thou and thy seed may live.

Deuteronomy 30:19

The greatest act of faith is when man decides he is not God.

*Know ye that the Lord he is God: it is he
that hath made us, and not we ourselves;
we are his people, and the sheep of his pasture.*

Psalm 100:3

Success is to be measured
not so much by the position
that one has reached in life
as by the obstacles which
he has overcome while
trying to succeed.

*Blessed is the man who perseveres under trial,
because when he has stood the test, he will receive the
crown of life that God has promised to those who love him.*

James 1:12 NIV

*T*o be upset over what you don't have is to waste what you do have.

Because the Lord is my Shepherd, I have everything I need!
Psalm 23:1 TLB

$\mathcal{A}$ true friend never gets in your way unless you happen to be going down.

A friend loves at all times, and a brother is born for adversity.
Proverbs 17:17 NASB

Laughter is the brush that sweeps away the cobwebs of the heart.

A happy heart is good medicine and a cheerful mind works healing, but a broken spirit dries up the bones.

Proverbs 17:22 AMP

*M*any a man thinks he has an open mind, when it's merely vacant.

...I warn everyone among you not to estimate and think of himself more highly than he ought [not to have an exaggerated opinion of his own importance]....

Romans 12:3 AMP

Character is not made in crisis, it is only exhibited.

I have set the Lord always before me: because he is at my right hand, I shall not be moved.

Psalm 16:8

Swallowing angry words before you say them is better than having to eat them afterwards.

*From the fruit of his mouth a man's
stomach is filled; with the harvest from his lips
he is satisfied. The tongue has the power of life
and death, and those who love it will eat its fruit.*

Proverbs 18:20,21 NIV

Happiness is a perfume
you cannot pour on
others without getting a
few drops on yourself.

━━•━━

Happy are those who long to be just and good,
for they shall be completely satisfied.

Matthew 5:6 TLB

Wisdom is the quality that keeps you from getting into situations where you need it.

I would have you learn this great fact: that a life of doing right is the wisest life there is. If you live that kind of life, you'll not limp or stumble as you run.

Proverbs 4:11,12 TLB

Rank does not confer privilege or give power. It imposes responsibility.

For everyone to whom much is given, of him shall much be required; and of him to whom men entrust much, they will require and demand all the more.

Luke 12:48b AMP

God has a history of using the insignificant to accomplish the impossible.

And Jesus looking upon them saith, With men it is impossible, but not with God: for with God all things are possible.

Mark 10:27

Depend on it, God's work done in God's way will never lack God's supplies.

*If you are willing and obedient,
you will eat the best from the land.*

Isaiah 1:19 NIV

*I*t's not how many hours you put in but how much you put into the hours.

Whatever you do, work at it with all your heart, as working for the Lord, not for men...It is the Lord Christ you are serving.

Colossians 3:23,24 NIV

A skeptic is a person who, when he sees the handwriting on the wall, claims it is a forgery.

The fool hath said in his heart, There is no God.

Psalm 14:1a

*T*wo things are bad for the heart — running up stairs and running down people.

*Let no corrupt communication proceed out
of your mouth, but that which is good to the use
of edifying, that it may minister grace unto the hearers.*

Ephesians 4:29

The trouble with most of us is that we would rather be ruined by praise than saved by criticism.

If you profit from constructive criticism you will be elected to the wise men's hall of fame. But to reject criticism is to harm yourself and your own best interests.

Proverbs 15:31,32 TLB

People may doubt what you say, but they will always believe what you do.

...for the tree is known and recognized and judged by its fruit.

Matthew 12:33 AMP

A professional is someone who can do his best work when he doesn't feel like it.

———

To win the contest you must deny yourselves many things that would keep you from doing your best.

1 Corinthians 9:25a TLB

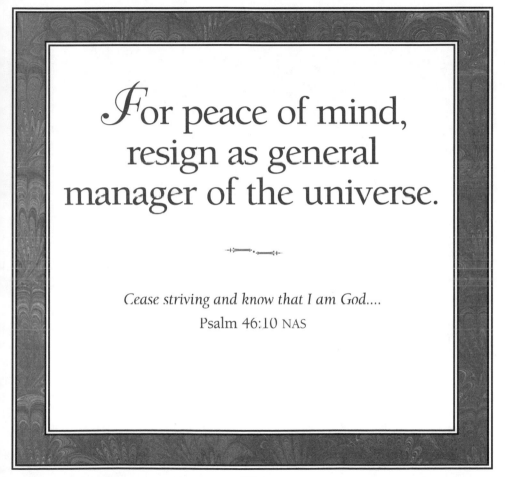

*F*or peace of mind,
resign as general
manager of the universe.

Cease striving and know that I am God....
Psalm 46:10 NAS

The best inheritance a parent can give to his children is a few minutes of his time each day.

Be very careful, then, how you live – not as unwise but as wise, making the most of every opportunity....

Ephesians 5:15,16 NIV

No one is useless in this world who lightens the burden of anyone else.

Now we who are strong ought to bear the weaknesses of those without strength and not just please ourselves. Let each of us please his neighbor for his good, to his edification.

Romans 15:1,2 NAS

Anger is a stone thrown at a wasp's nest.

Do not be quick in spirit to be angry or vexed,
for anger and vexation lodge in the bosom of fools.
Ecclesiastes 7:9 AMP

Wisdom is the wealth of the wise.

For the value of wisdom is far above rubies;
nothing can be compared with it.

Proverbs 8:11 TLB

*I*f you want to be a
leader with a large
following, just obey
the speed limit on a
winding, two-lane road.

<hr>

*Everyone has heard about your obedience, so I am full
of joy over you; but I want you to be wise about
what is good, and innocent about what is evil.*

Romans 16:19 NIV

Urgent things are seldom important. Important things are seldom urgent.

Every prudent man dealeth with knowledge....

Proverbs 13:16

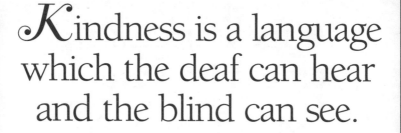

Kindness is a language which the deaf can hear and the blind can see.

For his merciful kindness is great toward us: and the truth of the Lord endureth for ever. Praise ye the Lord.

Psalm 117:2

People will be more impressed by the depth of your conviction than the height of your logic.

*My son, forget not my law; but let thine heart keep
my commandments...so shalt thou find favour
and good understanding in the sight of God and man.*

Proverbs 3:1,4

The most disappointed
people in the world
are those who get
what is coming to them.

A man's own folly ruins his life,
yet his heart rages against the Lord.
Proverbs 19:3 NIV

£ife affords no greater responsibility, no greater privilege, than the raising of the next generation.

Teach them (God's commandments) to your children,
talking about them when you sit at home and when you walk
along the road, when you lie down and when you get up...
So that your days and the days of your children may be many....

Deuteronomy 11:19,21 NIV

Compromise makes a good umbrella but a poor roof; it is a temporary expedient.

A good man is guided by his honesty;
the evil man is destroyed by his dishonesty.

Proverbs 11:3 TLB

People who fly into a rage always make a bad landing.

The discretion of a man deferreth his anger;
and it is his glory to pass over a transgression.

Proverbs 19:11

The right train of thought can take you to a better station in life.

For as he thinks within himself, so he is.
Proverbs 23:7a NAS

$\mathcal{L}$ife was a lot simpler
when we honored father
and mother rather than all
the major credit cards.

Children, obey your parents in the Lord, for this is right.
"Honor your father and mother" — which is the first
commandment with a promise — "that it may go well
with you and that you may enjoy long life on the earth."

Ephesians 6:1-3 NIV

Smart people speak
from experience —
smarter people from
experience, don't speak.

...he who restrains his lips is wise.
Proverbs 10:19 NASB

An atheist is a man who has no invisible means of support.

The fool hath said in his heart, There is no God.

Psalm 53:1a

A half-truth is usually less than half of that.

*The Lord detests lying lips,
but he delights in men who are truthful.*

Proverbs 12:22 NIV

I make it a rule of
Christian duty never
to go to a place where
there is not room for my
Master as well as myself.

*Don't be teamed with those who do not love the Lord...
How can a Christian be a partner with one who doesn't believe?*
2 Corinthians 6:14,15b TLB

*J*esus can turn water
into wine, but He can't
turn your whining
into anything.

Do all things without murmurings and disputings.
Philippians 2:14

Obstacles are those frightful things you see when you take your eyes off the goal.

And he (Jesus) said, Come. And when Peter was come down out of the ship, he walked on the water, to go to Jesus. But when he saw the wind boisterous, he was afraid; and beginning to sink, he cried, saying, Lord, save me. And immediately Jesus stretched forth his hand, and caught him....

Matthew 14:29-31

The price of greatness is responsibility.

But he that is greatest among you shall be your servant.

Matthew 23:11

Devoting a little of yourself to everything means committing a great deal of yourself to nothing.

———

Whatsoever thy hand findeth to do, do it with thy might....
Ecclesiastes 9:10

$\mathscr{A}$ diamond is a chunk of coal that made good under pressure.

Consider it all joy...when you encounter various trials, knowing that the testing of your faith produces endurance. And let endurance have its perfect result, that you may be perfect and complete, lacking in nothing.

James 1:2-4 NASB

The smallest deed is better than the greatest intention!

*...let us not love [merely] in theory or in speech
but in deed and in truth (in practice and in sincerity).*

1 John 3:18 AMP

The discipline of desire is the background of character.

But I keep under my body, and bring it into subjection:
lest that by any means, when I have preached to others,
I myself should be a castaway.

1 Corinthians 9:27

You can build a throne with bayonets, but you can't sit on it for long.

So are the ways of everyone who gains by violence;
it takes away the life of its possessors.

Proverbs 1:19 NASB

You can't fill an empty bucket with a dry well.

—•—

He who believes in Me, as the Scripture said, "From his innermost being shall flow rivers of living water."

John 7:38 NASB

I've suffered a great many
catastrophes
in my life. Most of
them never happened.

*For God hath not given us the spirit of fear;
but of power, and of love, and of a sound mind.*
2 Timothy 1:7

*H*appiness is the result of circumstances, but joy endures in spite of circumstances.

...in thy presence is fulness of joy; at thy right hand there are pleasures for evermore.

Psalm 16:11

One reason the dog has so many friends: he wags his tail instead of his tongue.

An evil man sows strife; gossip separates the best of friends.

Proverbs 16:28 TLB

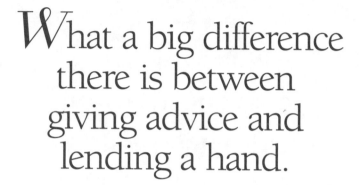

What a big difference there is between giving advice and lending a hand.

Little children, let us stop just saying we love people;
let us really love them, and show it by our actions.

1 John 3:18 TLB

The man who pays an ounce of principle for a pound of popularity gets badly cheated.

For they loved the praise of men more than the praise of God.
John 12:43

The heart has no secret which our conduct does not reveal.

The good man brings good things out of the good stored up in him, and the evil man brings evil things out of the evil stored up in him.

Matthew 12:35 NIV

Guilt is concerned with the past. Worry is concerned about the future. Contentment enjoys the present.

❖

Not that I am implying that I was in any personal want, for I have learned how to be content (satisfied to the point where I am not disturbed or disquieted) in whatever state I am.

Philippians 4:11 AMP

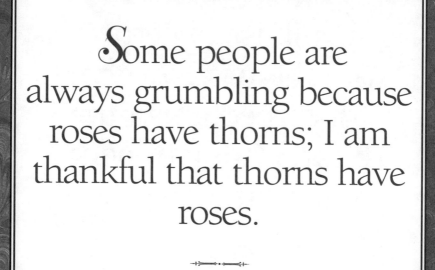

Some people are always grumbling because roses have thorns; I am thankful that thorns have roses.

Offer to God the sacrifice of thanksgiving....
Psalm 50:14 AMP

The next time you feel like complaining, remember that your garbage disposal probably eats better than 30 percent of the people in this world.

Let your conversation be without covetousness; and be content with such things as ye have....

Hebrews 13:5a

Our talks are often in first drafts — lots of corrections necessary!

⊹⊷•⊶⊹

For in many things we offend all. If any man offend not in word, the same is a perfect man, and able also to bridle the whole body.

James 3:2

Most of the shadows of this life are caused by standing in one's own sunshine.

A man's pride shall bring him low: but honour shall uphold the humble in spirit.

Proverbs 29:23

Death is not a period but a comma in the story of life.

⊷•⊶

Jesus said unto her (Martha), I am the resurrection, and the life: he that believeth in me, though he were dead, yet shall he live: And whosoever liveth and believeth in me shall never die.

John 11:25,26a

*T*o know the will of God
is the greatest knowledge,
to find the will of God is
the greatest discovery,
and to do the will of God
is the greatest achievement.

*If anyone serves Me, he must continue to follow Me [to cleave
steadfastly to Me, conform wholly to My example in living...] and
wherever I am, there will My servant be also. If anyone serves Me,
the Father will honor him.*

John 12:26 AMP

People with tact have less to retract.

—————

The heart of the righteous weighs its answers,
but the mouth of the wicked gushes evil.

Proverbs 15:28 NIV

*I*f the grass looks greener on the other side of the fence, you can bet the water bill is higher.

Let your character or moral disposition be free from love of money [including greed, avarice, lust, and craving for earthly possessions] and be satisfied with your present [circumstances and with what you have]....

Hebrews 13:5 AMP

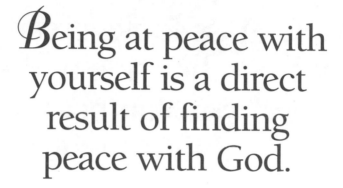

*B*eing at peace with
yourself is a direct
result of finding
peace with God.

*And the peace of God, which passeth all understanding,
shall keep your hearts and minds through Christ Jesus.*

Philippians 4:7

*I*f you want to make an easy job seem mighty hard, just keep putting off doing it.

***

...How long are ye slack to go to possess the land, which the Lord God of your fathers hath given you?

Joshua 18:3

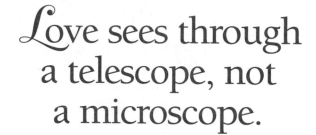

Love sees through a telescope, not a microscope.

Love endures long and is patient and kind...it takes no account of the evil done to it [it pays no attention to a suffered wrong].

1 Corinthians 13:4,5 AMP

Life is not a problem to be solved, but a gift to be enjoyed.

This is the day the Lord has made;
let us rejoice and be glad in it.

Psalm 118:24 NIV

*A*s I grow older,
I pay less attention to
what men say. I just
watch what they do.

*Show me your faith without deeds,
and I will show you my faith by what I do.*
James 2:18b NIV

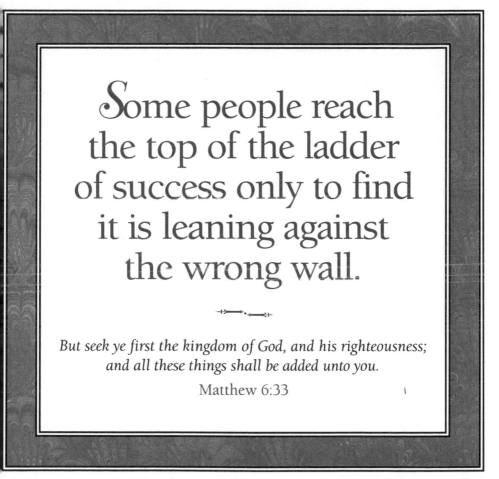

Some people reach
the top of the ladder
of success only to find
it is leaning against
the wrong wall.

*But seek ye first the kingdom of God, and his righteousness;
and all these things shall be added unto you.*

Matthew 6:33

$\mathcal{A}$ people who value its privileges above its principles soon lose both.

Uprightness and right standing with God (moral and spiritual rectitude in every area and relation) elevate a nation, but sin is a reproach to any people.

Proverbs 14:34 AMP

$\mathcal{A}$ pint of example is worth a barrelful of advice.

Brethren, join in following my example, and observe those who walk according to the pattern you have in us.

Philippians 3:17 NASB

*I*t has been my observation that most people get ahead during the time that others waste.

The plans of the diligent lead to profit as surely as haste leads to poverty.

Proverbs 21:5 NIV

*F*ear makes the wolf bigger than he is.

...though a mighty army marches against me, my heart shall know no fear! I am confident that God will save me.

Psalm 27:3 TLB

Beware lest your footprints on the sands of time leave only the marks of a heel.

The memory of the righteous will be a blessing, but the name of the wicked will rot.

Proverbs 10:7 NIV

The happiness of every country depends upon the character of its people, rather than the form of its government.

Happy is that people...whose God is the Lord.

Psalm 144:15

*I*n love, we may find
it better to make
allowances, rather
than make points.

Above all, love each other deeply,
because love covers over a multitude of sins.
1 Peter 4:8 NIV

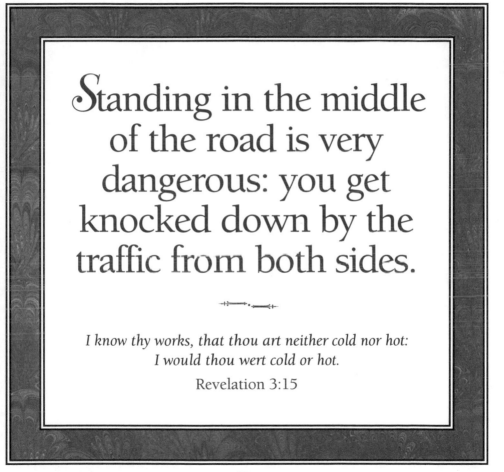

Standing in the middle of the road is very dangerous: you get knocked down by the traffic from both sides.

*I know thy works, that thou art neither cold nor hot:
I would thou wert cold or hot.*

Revelation 3:15

*I*f you were given a nickname descriptive of your character, would you be proud of it?

❦

A good name is rather to be chosen than great riches....
Proverbs 22:1a

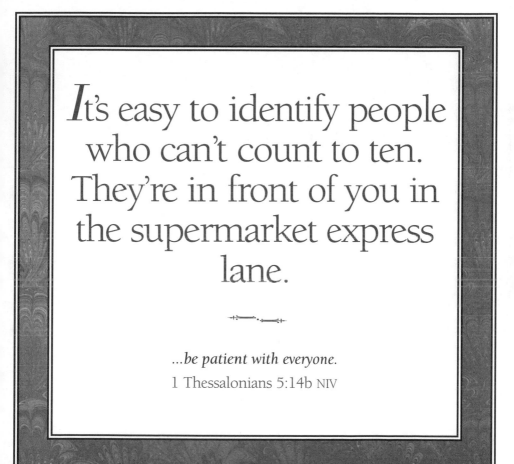

*I*t's easy to identify people who can't count to ten. They're in front of you in the supermarket express lane.

...be patient with everyone.
1 Thessalonians 5:14b NIV

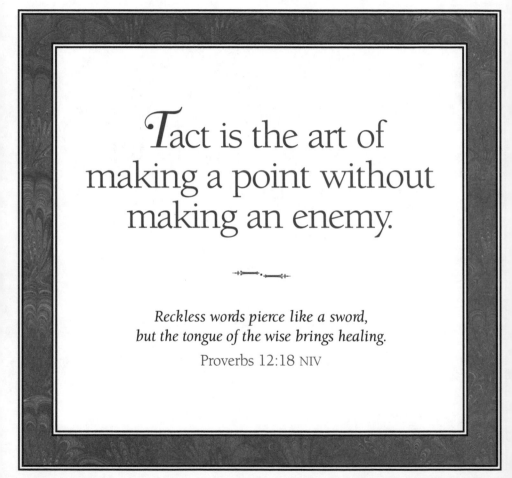

*T*act is the art of making a point without making an enemy.

*Reckless words pierce like a sword,
but the tongue of the wise brings healing.*

Proverbs 12:18 NIV

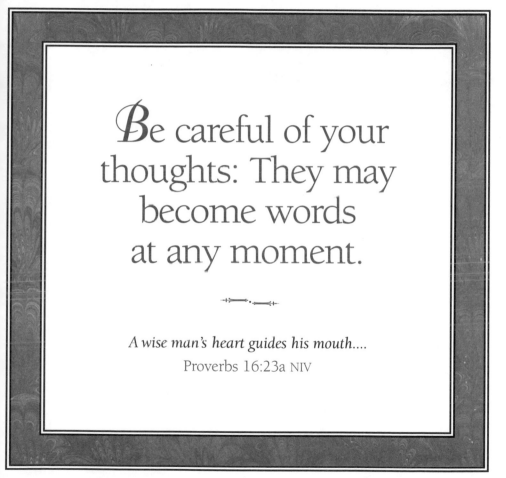

Be careful of your
thoughts: They may
become words
at any moment.

A wise man's heart guides his mouth....
Proverbs 16:23a NIV

*F*anatic: A person who's enthusiastic about something in which you have no interest.

Never be lacking in zeal,
but keep your spiritual fervor, serving the Lord.

Romans 12:11 NIV

*I*t is impossible for that man to despair who remembers that his Helper is omnipotent.

I lift up my eyes to the hills — where does my help come from?
My help comes from the Lord...The Lord will keep
you from all harm — he will watch over your life.

Psalm 121:1,2,7 NIV

Silence is one of the hardest arguments to refute.

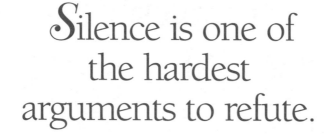

Whoso keepeth his mouth and his tongue keepeth his soul from troubles.

Proverbs 21:23

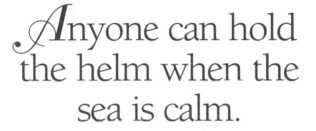

Anyone can hold the helm when the sea is calm.

If thou faint in the day of adversity, thy strength is small.
Proverbs 24:10

We learn from experience. A man never wakes up his second baby just to see it smile.

—⊷•⊷—

*The things you have learned and received
and heard and seen in me, practice these things;
and the God of peace shall be with you.*

Philippians 4:9 NASB

The best antique is an old friend.

———————

Your own friend and your father's friend,
forsake them not...Better is a neighbor who is near
[in spirit] than a brother who is far off [in heart].

Proverbs 27:10 AMP

Pray as if everything depended on God, and work as if everything depended upon man.

...faith without works is dead....
James 2:26

A good thing to remember, a better thing to do — work with the construction gang, not with the wrecking crew.

...When you meet together, each one has a hymn, a teaching, a disclosure of special knowledge or information, an utterance in a [strange] tongue, or an interpretation of it. [But] let everything be constructive and edifying and for the good of all.

1 Corinthians 14:26 AMP

*M*oney is a very excellent servant, but a terrible master.

Command those who are rich in this present world not to be arrogant nor to put their hope in wealth, which is so uncertain, but to put their hope in God, who richly provides us with everything for our enjoyment.

1 Timothy 6:17 NIV

If you can't feed
a hundred people,
then just feed one.

As we have therefore opportunity, let us do good unto all men....

Galatians 6:10

The trouble with stretching the truth is that it's apt to snap back.

*A false witness shall not be unpunished,
and he that speaketh lies shall not escape.*

Proverbs 19:5

Birthdays are good for you. Statistics show that the people who have the most live the longest.

So teach us to number our days,
that we may apply our hearts unto wisdom.
Psalm 90:12

*H*eaven goes by favor;
if it went by merit,
you would stay out, and
your dog would go in.

*For it is by free grace (God's unmerited favor)
that you are saved....*

Ephesians 2:8a AMP

A blind man who sees is better than a seeing man who is blind.

But blessed are your eyes, for they see: and your ears, for they hear.

Matthew 13:16

*I*f the roots are deep and strong, the tree needn't worry about the wind.

...blessed is the man who trusts in the Lord...He will be like a tree planted by the water that sends out its roots by the stream. It does not fear when heat comes; its leaves are always green. It has no worries in a year of drought and never fails to bear fruit.

Jeremiah 17:7,8 NIV

*M*en occasionally
stumble over the truth,
but most of them
pick themselves up
and hurry off as if
nothing happened.

The ear that heareth the reproof of life abideth among the wise.
Proverbs 15:31

Character is much easier kept than recovered.

...in speech, conduct, love, faith and purity,
show yourself an example of those who believe.
1 Timothy 4:12 NAS

$\mathcal{F}$aults are thick where love is thin.

And above all things have fervent charity among yourselves: for charity shall cover the multitude of sins.

1 Peter 4:8

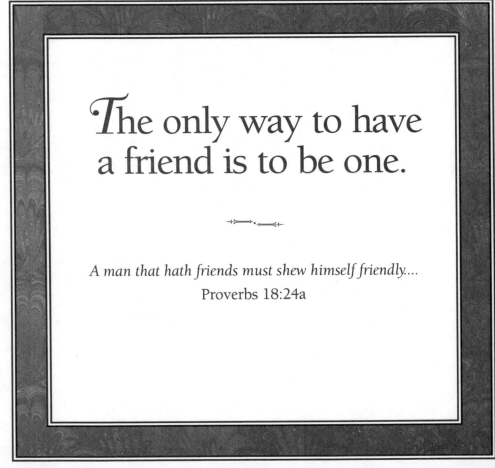

The only way to have a friend is to be one.

A man that hath friends must shew himself friendly....
Proverbs 18:24a

The world wants your best, but God wants your all.

...Thou shalt love the Lord thy God with all thy heart,
and with all thy soul, and with all thy mind.

Matthew 22:37

*H*indsight explains the injury that foresight would have prevented.

Do not forsake wisdom, and she will protect you...
When you walk, your steps will not be hampered;
when you run, you will not stumble.

Proverbs 4:6,12 NIV

Greatness lies not in being strong, but in the right use of strength.

...be strong in the Lord, and in the power of his might.
Ephesians 6:10

Do not in the darkness of night, what you'd shun in broad daylight.

The night is far spent, the day is at hand: let us therefore cast off the works of darkness, and let us put on the armour of light.

Romans 13:12

*I*f silence is golden, not many people can be arrested for hoarding.

———

In the multitude of words there wanteth not sin:
but he that refraineth his lips is wise.

Proverbs 10:19

Personality has the power to open doors, but character keeps them open.

The righteous shall never be removed....
Proverbs 10:30a

*A*uthority without wisdom is like a heavy axe without an edge, fitter to bruise than polish.

A ruler who lacks understanding is...a great oppressor.
Proverbs 28:16a AMP

Only when we have knelt before God, can we stand before men.

Humble yourselves therefore under the mighty hand of God, that he may exalt you in due time.

1 Peter 5:6

By perseverance the snail reached the Ark.

...let us run with perseverance the race marked out for us.

Hebrews 12:1b NIV

The worst moment for
the atheist is when he is
really thankful
and has nobody to thank.

Only a fool would say to himself, "There is no God."
Psalm 53:1a TLB

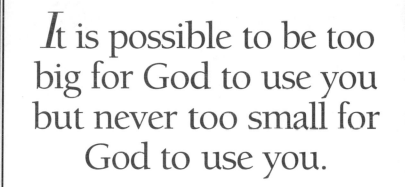

It is possible to be too big for God to use you but never too small for God to use you.

A man's pride brings him low, but a man of lowly spirit gains honor.

Proverbs 29:23 NIV

$\mathcal{K}$indness gives birth to kindness.

———•———

A kind man benefits himself,
but a cruel man brings trouble on himself.

Proverbs 11:17 NIV

*H*onesty is the first chapter of the book of wisdom.

Provide things honest in the sight of all men.
Romans 12:17b

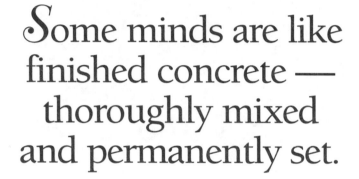

Some minds are like
finished concrete —
thoroughly mixed
and permanently set.

*Only by pride cometh contention:
but with the well advised is wisdom.*

Proverbs 13:10

*I*t is not guided missiles, but guided morals, that is our great need today.

The man of integrity walks securely....
Proverbs 10:9a NIV

The first rule of holes: When you're in one, stop digging.

He lifted me out of the slimy pit...he set my feet on a rock and gave me a firm place to stand. He put a new song in my mouth, a hymn of praise to our God.

Psalm 40:2,3 NIV

Deeds, not stones, are the true monuments of the great.

...let your light shine before men, that they may see your good deeds and praise your Father in heaven.

Matthew 5:16 NIV

God always gives His best to those who leave the choice with Him.

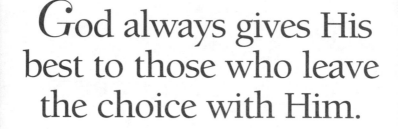

Blessed be the Lord, who daily loadeth us with benefits, even the God of our salvation.

Psalm 68:19

A Christian must keep the faith, but not to himself.

...Go ye into all the world, and preach the gospel to every creature.

Mark 16:15

A lot of people mistake a short memory for a clear conscience.

*And herein do I exercise myself, to have always
a conscience void of offense toward God, and toward men.*

Acts 24:16

*F*aith is not belief without proof, but trust without reservation.

...I know whom I have believed, and am persuaded that he is able to keep that which I have committed unto him against that day.

2 Timothy 1:12b

You can always tell a real friend: When you've made a fool of yourself he doesn't feel you've done a permanent job.

———•———

He who covers and forgives an offense seeks love, but he who repeats or harps on a matter separates even close friends.

Proverbs 17:9 AMP

$\mathcal{A}$ day hemmed in prayer is less likely to unravel.

...pray about everything; tell God your needs and don't forget to thank him for his answers. If you do this you will experience God's peace...His peace will keep your thoughts and your hearts quiet and at rest....

Philippians 4:6,7 TLB

Sandwich every bit of criticism between two layers of praise.

...correct, rebuke and encourage –
with great patience and careful instruction.
2 Timothy 4:2b NIV

When you flee temptations don't leave a forwarding address.

Now flee from youthful lusts, and pursue righteousness, faith, love and peace, with those who call on the Lord from a pure heart.
2 Timothy 2:22 NASB

*H*e who provides for
this life, but takes no
care for eternity,
is wise for a moment,
but a fool forever.

*What is a man profited, if he shall gain
the whole world, and lose his own soul?
or what shall a man give in exchange for his soul?*

Matthew 16:26

*M*orality may keep you out of jail, but it takes the blood of Jesus Christ to keep you out of hell.

In him we have redemption through his blood, the forgiveness of sins....

Ephesians 1:7a NIV

Courage is contagious. When a brave man takes a stand, the spines of others are stiffened.

...stand firm in the faith; be men of courage; be strong.
1 Corinthians 16:13b NIV

A coincidence is a small miracle where God prefers to remain anonymous.

Who can put into words and tell the mighty deeds of the Lord? Or who can show forth all the praise [that is due Him]?

Psalm 106:2 AMP

*A*t times, it is better
to keep your mouth
shut and let people
wonder if you're a fool
than to open it and
remove all doubt.

Even a fool, when he holdeth his peace,
is counted wise: and he that shutteth his lips
is esteemed a man of understanding.

Proverbs 17:28

Put not your trust in money, but put your money in trust.

***

Trust in your money and down you go!
Trust in God and flourish as a tree!
Proverbs 11:28 TLB

The man who sings his own praises always gets the wrong pitch.

Let another man praise thee, and not thine own mouth;
a stranger, and not thine own lips.

Proverbs 27:2

Sometimes the Lord calms the storm; sometimes He lets the storm rage and calms His child.

And the peace of God, which transcends all understanding, will guard your hearts and your minds in Christ Jesus.

Philippians 4:7 NIV

Blame yourself as you would blame others; excuse others as you would excuse yourself.

*Therefore, however you want
people to treat you, so treat them....*
Matthew 7:12a NASB

The past should be a springboard, not a hammock.

—⊷·⊶—

...but this one thing I do, forgetting those things which are behind, and reaching forth unto those things which are before.

Philippians 3:13b

*M*otivation is when your dreams put on work clothes.

Whatever you do, work at it with all your heart, as working for the Lord, not for men.

Colossians 3:23 NIV

The teacher asked the pupils to tell the meaning of loving-kindness. A little boy jumped up and said, "Well, if I was hungry and someone gave me a piece of bread, that would be kindness. But if they put a little jam on it, that would be loving-kindness."

Bless the Lord, O my soul...who crowneth thee with lovingkindness and tender mercies; who satisfieth thy mouth with good things....

Psalm 103:1,4,5

Our faith should be our steering wheel, not our spare tire.

...but the righteous will live by his faith.
Habakkuk 2:4 NIV

Others can stop you temporarily — you are the only one who can do it permanently.

Do you not know that in a race all the runners run, but only one gets the prize? Run in such a way as to get the prize.
1 Corinthians 9:24 NIV

Knowing and not doing are equal to not knowing at all.

*Therefore, to one who knows the right thing to do,
and does not do it, to him it is sin.*

James 4:17 NASB

Consider the turtle. He makes progress only when he sticks his neck out.

"Lord, if it's you," Peter replied, "tell me to come to you on the water." "Come," he (Jesus) said. Then Peter got down out of the boat, walked on the water and came toward Jesus.

Matthew 14:28,29 NIV

You can't act like a skunk without someone getting wind of it.

⊹⊱•⊰⊹

A good man out of the good treasure of the heart bringeth forth good things: and an evil man out of the evil treasure bringeth forth evil things.

Matthew 12:35

No man knows his true character until he has run out of gas, purchased something on the installment plan and raised an adolescent.

Consider it all joy, my brethren, when you encounter various trials, knowing that the testing of your faith produces endurance.

James 1:2,3 NASB

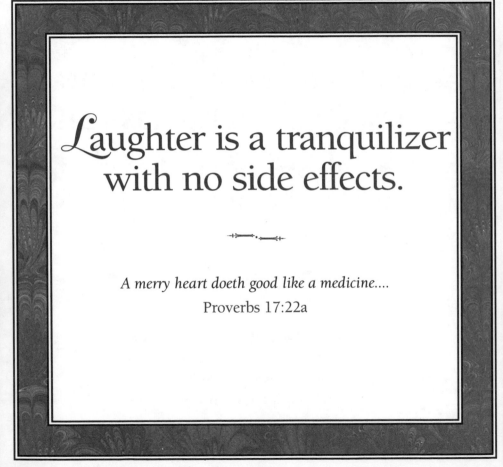

Laughter is a tranquilizer with no side effects.

A merry heart doeth good like a medicine....
Proverbs 17:22a

*I*t's not your outlook but your "uplook" that counts.

⟞·⟝

*Behold, as the eyes of servants look unto the hand
of their masters, and as the eyes of a maiden unto the hand
of her mistress; so our eyes wait upon the Lord our God....*
Psalm 123:2a

$\mathcal{A}$ winner makes commitments; a loser makes promises.

——•——

Lord, who may dwell in your sanctuary? He whose walk is blameless...who keeps his oath even when it hurts.

Psalm 15:1a,2,4 NIV

*I*t is reported that Moody's farewell words to his sons as he lay upon his deathbed were: "If God be your partner, make your plans large."

❧

I can do all things through Christ which strengtheneth me.

Philippians 4:13

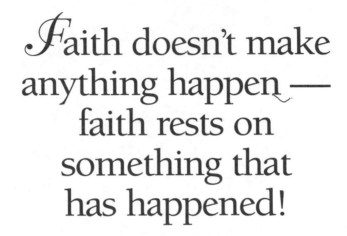

Faith doesn't make anything happen — faith rests on something that has happened!

My soul finds rest in God alone; my salvation comes from him.

Psalm 62:1 NIV

God never asks about our ability or our inability — just our availability.

———

I heard the voice of the Lord, saying, Whom shall I send, and who will go for us? Then said I, Here am I; send me.

Isaiah 6:8

Whenever a man is ready to uncover his sins, God is always ready to cover them.

—✦—

He that covereth his sins shall not prosper: but whoso confesseth and forsaketh them shall have mercy.

Proverbs 28:13

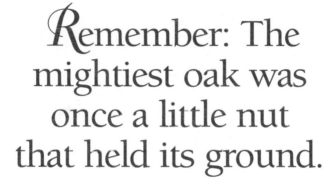

Remember: The mightiest oak was once a little nut that held its ground.

*Though your beginning was insignificant,
yet your end will increase greatly.*

Job 8:7 NASB

What is moral is what you feel good after.

———•———

Blessed are the pure in heart: for they shall see God.
Matthew 5:8

*I*f you're heading in the wrong direction, God allows u-turns.

...If you repent, I will restore you that you may serve me....
Jeremiah 15:19 NIV

Additional copies of this book and other titles
in the *God's Little Instruction Book* series
are available at your local bookstore.

God's Little Instruction Book
God's Little Instruction Book II
God's Little Instruction Book for Mom
God's Little Instruction Book for Dad
God's Little Instruction Book for Graduates
God's Little Instruction Book for Students
God's Little Instruction Book — Special Gift Edition
God's Little Instruction Book Daily Calendar

P.O. Box 55388
Tulsa, OK 74155